BOOKS FOR KIDS

Ultimate Minecraft Fart Warrior

3

From Book 1: A Hilarious fantasy for Minecrafting kids who love Farts!

What happens when a kid and his brother from Minecraft end up challenging each other in an Epic Fart Battle? Lots of chaos, jealousy and drama. Go on an epic adventure with two brothers Aiming to be the ULTIMATE FART KING!

Are you sure you can fart better than me?

If you love Fart Battles this is for you:
http://amzn.to/2qYiLXn

Check out my series and let me know what books you would like to read next.

Check out my page here: http://amzn.to/2p60OHJ

Table of Contents

The Ultimate Fart Warrior Competition

MONDAY MORNING

My weekend was as uneventful as most others, I worked my mine and took care of my animals. But somehow as I woke today the world felt different. I could almost hear a voice from above saying, "Steve, you are the man. You are the one to make a difference."

Only problem was I wasn't sure what difference I could make. I mean, I am the best mountain climber in all the area. That may sound a little too bold, buy hey, it is the truth. So exactly, what can a master mountain climber do to change the world?

My real moment of reflection was interrupted by a rumble in my stomach, and I knew what was going to follow that all too familiar noise. I prepared for the release of a fart that would most definitely be a dandy.

I was not disappointed as the sound echoed all around my house and even into the yard where Ol' Cowie Bunga was waiting for me to feed him. Poor Ol' Cowie must have thought the world was ending because he jumped and ran for the trees.

MONDAY NOON

I gathered supplies to cook lunch. My friends were all coming to my house just like they always do on Mondays. I love Mondays. They mean friends, fun, and games.

My mind was occupied on the crafting table as I was looking through my inventory. I didn't even hear, Alex and Sally sneak up behind me until they grabbed me. The shock hit my stomach like a brick and the rumbling of the morning came back with full force.

"Grrrrrrrr, ungh, grrrr." It was as if the bubbles in my stomach were zombies searching for victims. Maybe that is where the mini mooks begin. Haha, I chuckled to myself as the rumbling got louder and more intense. I didn't want to fart in front of the girls, but it might not be under my control.

"Hey, Steve, how're things going?" Alex's face got twisted as she heard the loud rumbling and I could see she wondered what it was. "Hey, you guys hear that? What is it?" Alex turned to Sally and looked all around for what was making that sound.

As my stomach roared with the rumble, I stepped closer to my trusty Mooshroom and hoped that the girls would blame him for what was coming. Strangely enough, the fart was just a little toot, and I don't think anyone even heard. That is except, Cowie Bunga, he heard it again, and I believe he thought another powerful one was going to follow. He jumped straight up in the air and ran for the trees again.

Sally grinned because she knew what it was, I should have been embarrassed, but I wasn't. She is a great friend and tried to change the subject to save my pride. "Oh, I don't know maybe some random zombies are creeping around. Hey, have you guys heard about the robbery in town?"

I hadn't heard anything about any robbery and was very curious. Sally told us that someone had stolen a chest full of diamonds and emeralds from Ivor, the keeper of the jewels.

My mind was trying to comprehend just how much those diamonds and emeralds were worth when I heard the loud voices of my buddies. Luke, Axel, and my cousin, Jesse were running toward us with their arms waving like they were on fire.

I stepped back wondering what the devil was wrong. They all spoke at the same time, and it is hard to make any sense of the noise.

"Hey, guys, come on. One at a time." I barely got the words out of my mouth with their excitement reaching such a level.

"Steve, you will never guess what is happening in town." Jesse was always excited, but today he was red with excitement.

"What is it?" I asked them. I was curious what could make them all act this way.

"They are having a competition for Ultimate Fart Warrior of the whole Overworld!"

Okay, I wasn't sure if I had heard that correctly. I thought Jesse said, Ultimate Fart Warrior.

I couldn't even reply before Sally muttered under her breath. "Well, Steve would be great in that contest."

Shrugging my shoulders, I tried to ignore her snarky words, but I knew she was right. "What on earth is the Ultimate Fart Warrior?" I turned all my attention to my buddies hoping that Sally would stop her jabs about my farting.

But when I think about it, if anyone was the Ultimate Fart Warrior, well, it was me. I could out fart all of these guys.

I shook my head because I am not sure that is a reason to be proud.

Everyone gathered around the table as we began to eat and we talked about the strange contest. Who in the world came up with this idea about an Ultimate Fart Warrior? Seriously, was it just a joke or what?

MONDAY NIGHT

Axel moved toward the window, and I could tell that he was making the same move I always did when a fart was coming. His face got that certain look when you know you are going to fart and don't want to call attention to yourself.

Just as he raised his foot to let the fart loose, Alex stepped up beside him. The fart met her nose almost instantly. It was hilarious.

"Oh, my gosh Axel. What on earth? Did you eat that?" Alex pinched her nose as she moved away from Axel and the stench as fast as she could.

Everyone laughed so hard we all nearly cried.

MONDAY NIGHT (In Bed)

I lay staring at the ceiling thinking about what Jesse had said about this weird contest. I had never heard that the elders of town had found out that certain powerful farts were a good defense against not only Creepers but Witches.

Just thinking about farts being a weapon was so weird, I fell asleep as images of farts floating in my head.

TUESDAY MORNING

I got up earlier than my friends and prepared our breakfast. As always, they all woke up just when I finished with the food. You would think they did it on purpose, that way they didn't have to cook.

Our conversation consisted on the subject of farts. Big farts, loud farts, little toot farts, and those ever annoying silent farts. No one knew why farts were such a powerful weapon against the zombies, but we all had opinions about different reasons.

Before we headed out to join the contest, I snuck out of my house and ate a bunch of pork, beef, and as much beetroot soup as I could get past my lips. I don't like the soup. It makes me super gassy. But hey, that was what I needed to be before a fart contest.

My mind still couldn't wrap around the idea of a contest for the best farter. Oh well, I thought I had seen everything after seeing The Wither last winter. Now, I know that thought was wrong. So terribly wrong.

TUESDAY NOON

The walk into town should have thrilled me because the woods always make me happy. I love seeing the madrone trees with their vibrant orange color. Boy, what I could do with that wood. And today with the mixture of the red, golden colored leaves of the sugar maples and the blue spruce standing in all their glory among the maples and madrone, all those trees just blurred in my vision. All I could think about was farting.

Would I fart loud enough? Would my farts be robust, sufficient to stop a Witch? Or would I wimp out and only muster up a little toot? OH, my gosh, what if I couldn't fart at all?

Sadly, thoughts of the elusive master fart of the entire world were filling my head as I stumbled into Jesse who had stopped right in front of me. I didn't even notice him until I was lying on the ground looking up.

"Jesse, what the.," I muttered at my favorite cousin, who at that moment was just staring into the sky.

"Did you hear that?" Jesse continued to look up like he saw something.

Axel helped me up as he told Jesse he heard nothing. The girls came running back to us. I hadn't even noticed they had gotten so far ahead.

Sally walked to Jesse and looked up, a very puzzled look on her face. She started to say something but stopped when we all saw what Jesse was watching. It was the largest group of bats any of us had ever seen. They were coming from a spot on the mountain that everyone knew only had Zombies, Creepers, and a group of Witches.

No one had ever seen bats in that area, so it was weird.

Rising from the ground, I watched the bats with just a little fear. I know deep down in my mind that the bats don't hurt you, but there was a large part of me that didn't want them to get tangled in all my Fabio hair. It was a lot of work to look like this, and I sure didn't want those bats to mess it up.

I never realized that I had covered my head with both arms until the girls began to laugh.

"Oh, my gosh, Steve. Seriously, you and that hair." Alex laughed so hard she fell over on the ground, and Sally doubled up in her laughter.

"Stop it. You guys know you love it when I look like Fabio. So just cool your giggles." I brushed the hair back with one quick sweep of my hands. I didn't want to look at my buddies. I knew they didn't feel the same way. They said they thought I looked like a doofus, but I still believe that they are just jealous. I mean I pull off this look so well.

All the attention on my hair pulled us away from the thoughts of the bats. We walked toward town not thinking any more about why the bats were acting weird.

TUESDAY AFTERNOON (TOWN)

The crowded streets filled with people, as everyone gathered for the first contest of the season. The one thing this town liked more than anything was competition. It didn't matter what the contest was, as long as we could compete.

It was only last month that I had won the contest for best mountain climber and I was still riding high from the glory.

Walking through the crowd, I could hear shouts of "Hey, Steve!" filling the air. I held my head up with so much pride. Jesse kept whispering that I had better be careful, cause if it rained, I would drown.

He was just jealous, cause I was 'The Man' and he wasn't.

Both Axel and Jesse laughed as I pushed my way in front of the group. After all, I needed to greet my fans. Sure, I was kind of a jerk about it, but it was fun.

We moved past most of the people making our way up to the front where we got a better look of the ones competing right now. No one had a chance to fart when the Mayor stepped to the podium.

The Mayor straightened his tie and let out a roaring fart. "brrr RTT TTT!" It was loud, and it was stinky. His laughter mixed in the air with the stench. "I guess I should be competing today after that exhibition!"

The crowd laughed with a boisterous laugh. That sound mixed in the air with sounds of farts all around. There was almost a green tint to the air with all the release of gasses. It was funny and wrong all at the same time.

Raising his hand, the Mayor, motioned for everyone to quiet down. "Now, let the town of Garrison begin the first annual Ultimate Fart Warrior competition. My the gassiest win." The crowd roared.

Stepping up to the podium one after another, people farted their best farts. There was big farts, loud farts, little toot farts, and some farts that made you flinch from the smell, but the line continued one after another.

TUESDAY AFTERNOON

(Ultimate Fart Warrior Contest)

I stood in line among so many people, each of us waiting for the opportunity to fart. I couldn't even count them all. Each of them farting here and there as they practiced for their chance at the title of Ultimate Fart Warrior.

My stomach rumbled and growled as the smell filtered across my nose. I don't know if I have ever smelt anything this bad. Especially not like the rank air around this group of people. I listened to all the conversations about the diamond and emerald heist, theories about who had done the robbery ran from the Mayor to the Sheriff. People began to think their neighbors had stolen the jewels.

Sure, I guess you had to admit that this was the biggest robbery this town had ever seen and combined with this great stink contest the town was hopping.

"Hey, fella who you think is the thief?"

I barely heard the words as I still tried to imagine how on earth a fart was going to defeat any Zombies. Do they smell the rank air and just fall over dead? Or what? That is such a weird theory. I wonder who came up with the idea.

"Hey, I was talking to you." The man, I recognized as Sigga hit me on the shoulder.

Jerking back to look him in the eye, I tried to listen to him.

"I asked who you thought was the thief?"

I shook my head. I started to answer his question as my stomach rumbled so loud it was like a wolf growling. "Grrrrrrr, ugh, grrrr." I held my stomach hoping that the fart of all farts would wait just a little while longer. After all, if I was going to let one rip in front of all these people I wanted it to be the granddaddy of all farts.

Laughing Sigga leaned his body to the side and farted. It was a decent enough fart, just not as loud as he thought it was.
"Yes sir, right there is the fart of the Ultimate Warrior. I got this contest in the bag."

I couldn't even say anything. His fart might not have been the loudest but boy it was one of the rankest I had ever smelled. I held my nose as he laughed and laughed.

Our conversation on the robbery got lost in all the smell, and I turned back to the podium.
The Mayor walked back up and held his hands in the air.

"If I could have everyone's attention, please." The Mayor waited for the crowd to stop talking before he spoke. "There has been questions about the use of farts as weapons. And for the answer, I have a guest speaker to explain. Please welcome, Magnus the Magnificent."

Stepping aside the Mayor allowed the face that everyone knew, it was a hero that had saved our town many times.

TUESDAY AFTERNOON

(MAGNUS THE MAGNIFICENT SPEECH)

"Ahem, thank you Mr. Mayor. Now for those who wonder why we think that a fart can be used as a weapon, I stand as proof. You see, just a short time ago I found myself pinned down with a hundred Zombies bearing in for the kill. I was injured, and I had lost my sword in the previous fight." Magnus paused as the crowd gasped. "That was when, well, I farted. Now, I know that is not usually something you think about when you think of us, heroes. But the truth is we fart, too."

The crowd laughed at the humor and thought of Magnus the Magnificent farting as the Zombies attacked. I leaned forward not wanting to miss a word. This theory of a fart weapon was fascinating to me.

"When I farted it was as if a bomb had exploded. The Zombies fell dead. They didn't spawn again, and there was no rotten meat left behind. It was just as if they had never existed. They were gone."

There was a hush that fell over the crowd. This was fantastic. I wondered if it made the Zombies just disappear, what did it do to Creepers and Witches? Others must have wondered the same thing because I could hear the question repeated over and over.

Waving his hands to calm everyone, Magnus continued. "Yes, I know you wonder about the effect on other creatures. And the answer is yes. It works on them all. I have seen with my own eyes what happens."

Okay, so my question was answered, but then I had another. Stepping in front of the line, I cleared my voice and spoke. "Magnus, if you have used it yourself, why do you need an Ultimate Warrior?"

"Yes, yes, we want to know. Why Magnus?" The people all echoed my question as we waited for the answer. Lowering his head, I could see Magnus swallow uncomfortably. "Well, I have been treated by the doctor, and I sadly can no longer fart."

What? That was possible? I couldn't believe it. Jesse nudged me as he was thinking the same thing and I could see the confusion go over Axel's face as well.

While Magnus stepped away from the podium in embarrassment, the Mayor made his way back in front of the crowd.
I wasn't sure if the Mayor had spoken yet or not, I was so intrigued by the fact that our hero was embarrassed

that he COULDN'T fart. Weren't we usually embarrassed that we farted? How weird is this?

The Mayor thanked Magnus for his participation and for all the things he had done for our beloved town. Then, with a swing of his arm, the parade of farting continued.

TUESDAY AFTERNOON
(IN LINE FOR THE CONTEST)

The line seemed to move slow as I held my stomach hoping that my farts would wait just a few minutes longer. While I waited, I looked across the crowd for the girls.

I finally spotted them sitting far from the podium with their noses held. They were rooting for Axel and me to do good in our farting attempts. I could see in their faces that they really would have preferred to be anywhere but here.

There was a part of me that found it hilarious that they were stuck on this beautiful day watching a bunch of people fart. Who would have thought that would ever happen?

As I focused on my friends, my stomach let loose, and the smallest fart in the history of the world escaped. It left a tiny little, 'toot, toot' that caused all the people around me to burst out laughing.

Strangely enough, I was so embarrassed. What a puny little fart. They all thought that was all I had in me and continued to make fun of the little fart man.

I gritted my teeth and felt the rumblings in my stomach ache to release the one fart I knew I was holding inside. And it was so hard not just to let it rip. But it wasn't time yet.

"Don't let them bug you, Steve. Axel and I know how great you can fart. Just let them have their fun and forget about it." Jesse did what he had done since we were kids, he tried to make me feel better.

"It's alright, Jesse. I know what I can do. I just wish you would give it a try too." I knew my cousin was terrified about being in front of a crowd and I knew that was why he didn't want to try.

"No, I 'm good. I don't want to be any ultimate warrior." Jesse chuckled a nervous little giggle as he moved to the side.
I was next in line to give it my farting best. Oh crap, why was my stomach settling down? Would I be able to fart when the time came? Was I an Ultimate Fart Warrior?

The guy ahead of me strained with all his might making his face as red as an apple. I thought for sure he was going to pass out when finally he farted.

'toot.'

That was it. His fart was even smaller than the tiny little toot that caused everyone to laugh at me. Oh man, I felt real bad for him. He was still straining with everything he had, and there was just nothing. Not one single little toot to follow. No hiss, nothing. It was kind of sad watching him try to fart so hard.

Wobbling against the podium the guy strained again and again, yet nothing happened. He strained until he fell on the podium again almost passing out. The Mayor stepped up to get him to go on and move aside.

"Well looks like he just hasn't got one in him. Ha ha." The Mayor motioned for me to move forward.

TUESDAY AFTERNOON

(MY TURN IN THE CONTEST)

I twisted my neck side to side, brushed my Fabio hair from my forehead and realized for the first time just how nervous I was. Why weren't my feet working? I looked down staring at what appeared to be someone else's feet. They just sat there. Okay, I told myself to snap out of it. This was the moment of truth. I knew I was a farting champion and now was time to show the world.

Come on, Steve. I told myself just to move one foot at a time. I could hear the girls scream my name and I could feel the eyes of my buddies watching me from behind. It was hard. Why is it so hard?

Finally, as if I woke from a dream my feet moved. One step and then another, finally I was at the podium.

Clearing my throat, I closed my eyes and prayed that my stomach would not let me down. Of all times, I wanted that familiar rumbling to kick in and take over.

It felt like hours as the rumble began to grow and grow. Finally, as the crowd was so quiet that you could hear a pin fall to the floor, the grumble and rumble hit its target.

"BRRRRRRRMMMMM RRRRRMMMMM GRRRRMMM"

Oh my gosh, I couldn't believe the echo. The silence was broken by what was the loudest sound I had ever heard. My fart, yes, it was my fart. But not only my fart, but it was also a fart that was the master to all other farts in the world.

The crowd went crazy. They screamed and chanted my name as Magnus rushed forward.

"I do believe we have a winner. Dude, that was incredible. It wouldn't surprise me if Zombies, Creepers, and Witches died for miles."

Magnus kept talking but somewhere after he said 'we have a winner' I stopped listening. My stomach felt so relieved after that massive fart that multitudes of smaller, but just as impressive, farts followed.

It was as if I was a one man band blaring music for the world to hear.

My friends came rushing forward, holding their noses. They were so proud of me, and I was still so shocked.

Our celebration continued as the people raised me in the air and began to pass me around above their heads. This was unreal. I, Steve, was now the ULTIMATE FART WARRIOR! How could this be? I mean, I had hoped, but I didn't think it would happen. This was so crazy. Completely, amazing, yet it was crazy.

"Steve, Steve, Steve, FART CHAMPION!!!" The words echoed through my head as I tried to focus. My mind was spinning with each chant. Then, it hit me.

If I am a Fart Warrior, I mean a warrior that can kill Zombies, Creepers, and other stuff, what did that mean? Was I to head out on quests to kill all the wrong things? What did they want me to do? IF I was always out on quests, who would take care of my home and Cowie Bunga? Crap, I hadn't given this much thought.

My mind began to get fuzzy as I tried to figure out what I was going to do. I was so intense on what I was supposed to do that I didn't see the Sheriff rush forward. With a loud whistle, the Sheriff stopped the celebration.

"Please, if everyone would please be quiet!" The Sheriff motioned for quiet, and he got just that.

Unfortunately, for me when the crowd got quiet I got dropped. With a loud thud, I hit the ground, HARD.

TUESDAY AFTERNOON (AFTER THE CONTEST THE SHERIFF SPEAKS)

"Please, I know everyone heard about the robbery. Well as you know the thieves took all the wealth of the town. Every diamond and every emerald. If we don't get it back well, we are finished as a town."

Gasps filled the air as the people realized the severity of the situation. People began yelling, "What do we do?"

The Sheriff swallowed as he spoke, "Well, the thieves have been spotted. They are stuck in the Zombie Zone." His words met horrified ears of a crowd that knew what went into the Zombie Zone never came out again.

"If we don't get those jewels back people, we are done."

The Sheriff turned slowly until he was eye to eye with me. He stepped toward me, and I knew what the consequences for my fart were now.

"Steve, as you are now Ultimate Fart Warrior, it is time to stand up to that name."

I was terrified. Not only did no one ever come back from the Zombie Zone but we all knew that there were thousands of Creepers, Witches, and Zombies just waiting for some unsuspecting fool to get close.

My heart raced as the crowd looked at me, I was nauseous. Sure I farted now, but could I muster a fart when I needed it the most?

Everyone began moving closer and closer to me, each of them had such expectations in their eyes. What in the world was I going to do?

"Steve." The Mayor made his way to me with Magnus by his side. "Steve looks like you are up."

I swallowed my heart as it threatened to jump out of my mouth. I wasn't ready for this. I didn't want this. My eyes searched Magnus' face, and I realized that he probably hadn't been completely honest with all of us. I saw the fear in his face, and I got even more terrified.

TUESDAY EVENING

The day had been fun, until now. Everyone stood waiting for me to head up the mountain. To the Zombie Zone.

I held my breath and quietly whispered low to myself. "Crap."

TUESDAY EVENING (AFTER the Contest)

My knees were shaking as if I were one of the skeletons. I wanted to be brave, but I was terrified. Never in my life have I done anything like what the ENTIRE town wanted me to do now.

I don't know what they are thinking. Me, Steve, the regular ordinary guy. Sure I was good-looking with my Fabio hair, but a Warrior? I was not sure about this. Me, mountain climber extraordinaire but Warrior? This has to be a mistake. Seriously, me Steve a Warrior?

My mind was racing with all of the dangers that could be waiting for me out there in the Zombie Zone, and it just kept building until I thought I would pass out.

The voices of the townspeople echoed, "Steve, Steve, Ultimate Fart Warrior!!!!" Over and over I heard all the shouting, but it wasn't helping at all.

"Crap." That was the only thing that would come out of my mouth. Crap, crap, crap. I just wanted to run away. Yeah, that is what I will do. RUN!

I turned toward the trees and started to make a break for them. But as my feet prepared to run, I heard Jesse. His voice seemed to come from the darkness that had overtaken my mind.

"Steve! You can do this."

Wow, how could he sound so sure? I mean, he knows me right? And yet, his voice sounded like he believed in my ability to be a Warrior.

"Steve, you can do this. I have had experience as a kind of warrior. Well, I have had quests before." Jesse's hand rested on my shoulder in a sort of spiritual connection. He was trying to send me strength to handle this thing called Fart Warrior.

Okay, come on Steve. I whispered this command to myself hoping that it would calm me down. Well, it did. How strange. Just moments ago I was ready to run for the hills and leave all of this warrior business in the dust.

Breath in, breath out. I just kept trying to calm my nerves and as I did my eyes began to focus enough that I saw all of my friends gathered around me. They looked so confident. Or maybe they were just trying to make me feel more confident. I don't know, but it was working.

"Steve, the town needs you to go and find our jewels.

We must have those diamonds and emeralds back or, well, this town is kaput." The Mayor reached out to shake my hand as I saw Magnus walking closer to me.

I opened my mouth wanting to say this was still all a colossal mistake, but the words got lost somewhere between my tongue and my lips. Instead, I heard a voice that sounded like my own. "Yes, Mayor. We have to get those diamonds and emeralds." A deep breath and that voice that I couldn't believe was mine continued. "I am going to form an army, a Fart Army."

Wow, where did that come from? It was genius. If, I had some back-up. Maybe just maybe I would be able to handle this quest to retrieve the jewels.

TUESDAY EVENING (My HOUSE)

The sun had begun to go down as my friends gathered around my kitchen table. Each of them had a look of wonder on their face as they waited for me to speak. Across the room, I saw Magnus, who had accompanied us here. He seemed eager to say something but somehow was afraid to open his mouth.

"Well, everyone this is what I want to do." I stopped, wondering if they would agree with my idea or would they run. Oh, well here goes nothing. "Guys, I want us to be the Fart Army."

The room got dark with silence as they just stared at me with open mouths. At least, all of them expect Jesse.

Wow, I was surprised. My little cousin, the one who was afraid to be in front of crowds, seemed to be a lot braver than I thought.

"Steve," Jesse stepped forward reaching his hand out to grip my shoulder. "Yes, I agree. It is always better to have more than one when you are facing a dangerous quest."

Crap, my little cousin was braver than me. Where did all of this come from? "Jesse, I am proud of you. When did you get so brave?"

He smiled the funniest grin I had ever seen and began to tell me his story. "You remember last year when you were gone? Well, I too, had a quest. Remember The Wither? The one that was threatening my town during the time of EnderCon. Well, we went on a quest to find it and destroy it."

I couldn't believe my ears, was this true? Could my Jesse, be THE Jesse I heard about? "What?"

Axel stepped up and said that it was true. Jesse was a hero, and he had been there when it happened. From across the room, I heard Magnus say the same thing.

Wow, I was blown away. I never knew.

The girls moved in closer as we talked about Jesse's quest and the creation of my new Fart Army.

"Steve," Sally's voice was small and almost too quiet to hear. "Steve, I want to be part of your army." She swallowed deeply before quickly adding. "I can fart, big too."

Her words stopped all of us right dead in our tracks. Was she admitting that as a girl, she could fart as big and loud as we could? Really?

"Don't look so shocked Steve." Alex was quick to jump in when she saw that we were having a real problem with the idea that girls fart as bad as guys do. "Yes, oh my gosh. We girls can fart too. Sometimes even bigger than you."

WEDNESDAY MORNING

The night had kept me from sleeping very much. I was thinking about what Sally and Alex had said about girls farting. I thought back to the day that Sally and I went mining. Maybe all the farts weren't just me. I had wondered then, about the one that formed the giant bubble. I mean, at the time it just seemed that it was me. But now? I am not so sure.

And, if Sally had done that fart. Well, she was qualified to join my Fart Army.

WEDNESDAY NOON

Our group, the newly formed Fart Army, gathered under the sugar maple tree in my yard. I stared at my garden. It was full of pumpkins, carrots, melons, and potatoes. If I went on this quest to the Zombie Zone would I see that little garden again?

As I wondered about my garden, my trusty friend, and companion, Cowie Bunga came ambling up to rub my arm. He was a strange little Mooshroom, but I do love him. He has always been such a good friend.

Maybe, it was the way that all of my friends looked at me. Perhaps, it was the way that Cowie Bunga made me feel. I don't know, but whatever it was, I felt secure. I felt able to do this. I felt like I WAS the Ultimate Fart Warrior.

WEDNESDAY NOON (FART ARMY GETTING READY TO LEAVE TOWN)

Here, we stood. Me, Steve, the Ultimate Fart Warrior, with my good and capable Fart Army. Jesse, my brave cousin, stood as my second in command. Axel, my overly large and slightly goofy, Sergeant at Arms, the girls, Sally and Alex, my loyal soldiers, and then in the back was Magnus the Magnificent. But somehow, he didn't seem so magnificent today.

The Mayor and the Sheriff stood to see us off on your journey to the Zombie Zone. With the entire town screaming our names and shouting how they were so happy we were going to save them. That was incredible.

I had finally begun to feel like being this Fart Warrior, might be a good thing. After all the town, I mean the WHOLE town, was here cheering us and they loved us. This felt pretty good.

We placed our supplies on the back of some good horses and laughed as we made sure there was plenty of beetroot soup. The disgusting stuff was a sure fire way to rumble my stomach into its strongest fighting position. This soup would be the best way to bring out the fart that would save us all.

I tied the straps around our supplies with the best knot I could and turned to the town one last time."Well, Mr. Mayor, Sheriff, we are off to get the diamonds and emeralds." Why, didn't those words sound stronger? In my head, it had been this powerful speech that everyone would cheer and remember forever. The words that I just said seemed, well weak.

It must not have mattered because they shook my hand and patted us all on the backs as they waved good-bye. Maybe they did not just wish us a safe journey, perhaps, just maybe they were bidding us farewell? Oh, crap. Where did those thoughts come from?

WEDNESDAY AFTERNOON
(ON THE ROAD TO THE ZOMBIE ZONE)

The horses carrying our supplies plodded along behind Axel and Jesse. The girls ran ahead laughing and jabbering like they were on their way to a party. I marched behind them all with Magnus just off to my side.

I looked at Magnus from the corner of my eye and saw he was kicking the dirt blocks as we walked. He was acting weird, and I figured this was as good a time as any to find out why."Hey, Magnus." He turned to face me, and I saw he was upset about something."What's wrong? Are you okay?" I stopped walking and leaned on a stone block. "Magnus, talk to me."

I could hear his shallow breathing as he stepped up closer. Sitting down on the stone blocks, he acted like he was made of lead. I knew right then that something was wrong, dreadful wrong.

"Come on Magnus, whatever is bothering you can't be as bad as you act. Tell me." I hoped that the soothing sound of my voice would reassure him and I could get to the bottom of this.

"Oh, Steve. Oh, Steve, I am so sorry."

Magnus was so upset. I think he was about to cry. Okay, so now he was beginning to freak me out and when I get scared my stomach goes into power rumbles. The gurgling and growling of my stomach echoed across the field where the rest of the group had gathered to feed the horses.

"GRRRRRR, grrrr." My stomach began to talk in a loud

roar. Oh, crap. Now isn't the time to worry about farting, so I just let whatever comes from this rumble have its way. My focus went back to Magnus.

"Steve, I don't know how to tell you this."

That grumble in my stomach decided this was the perfect time to release what sounded like a trumpet."Ferrum, mmmm. Grrrr boom." Even though this was a serious conversation between Magnus and me, I couldn't help but giggle at the sound of that fart. And the fact that I let it rip without even trying to cover it up. Wow, how times change in just a few days.

Trying to stop my childish giggles I bit my lip and tried to look serious. "Okay, Magnus. Whatever is bothering you can't be that bad. Surely, it isn't bad enough to make you this terrified to tell me. So just spit it out, man."

The rest of the group must have heard my fart or saw the look in Magnus' face. I don't know which one. Because they started walking toward us with worried looks on their faces. You would have thought there was a Zombie invasion right here,
"Steve," Magnus paused again.

Whatever it was he wanted to say, sure was difficult. I truly began to get annoyed. Come on man, just tell me already. At this rate, we would never get to the Zombie Zone.

"Steve, I have to tell you that, well, that...." His voice cracked as he saw everyone gather behind me."Crap, this is hard."

"Tell us, Magnus. This is getting serious." I hoped my voice didn't sound as mad as I felt. This whole hum hah thing was getting old.

"Steve, well you see, farts don't actually work."

WHAT?????

To be Continued...

FOLLOW THE NEXT RELEASE

In the meantime, Don't forget book 1 & 2…

Book 1 and 2 series: *http://amzn.to/2qYiLXn*

What happens when a kid and his brother from Minecraft end up challenging each other in an Epic Fart Battle? Lots of chaos, jealousy and drama. Go on an epic adventure with two brothers <u>Aiming to be the ULTIMATE FART KING</u>!

Are you sure you can fart better than me?

If you love Fart Battles this is for you: http://amzn.to/2qYiLXn

Check out my series and let me know what books you would like to read next.

Check out my page here: http://amzn.to/2p60OHJ

Other Authors that I like:

Nooby Lee writes some of the BEST diaries as Roblox, feel free to check him out
http://amzn.to/2pZBVvY

Series by Marc Emerson: Beyond Good and Evil, which are You?

Go Here to download: http://amzn.to/2nd8KpD

Check the series: http://amzn.to/2pXHJYQ

Other Authors that I like:

"Diary Of A Wimpy Super Mario" series

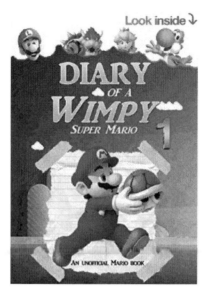

Click here to get it ➔ *http://amzn.to/2ejL6nT*

In this book, you will meet Mario, the wimpy Plumber with his brother Luigi and their Adventures in saving the Princess. Will Mario be able to change his Wimpiness and save the Princess?

Click here to get Wimpy Mario Book 2 ➔ *http://amzn.to/2dFWls4*

Wimpy Mario Book 3 ➔ *http://amzn.to/2dqNNA5*

Are you a Zelda Fan? Then Check out some of these

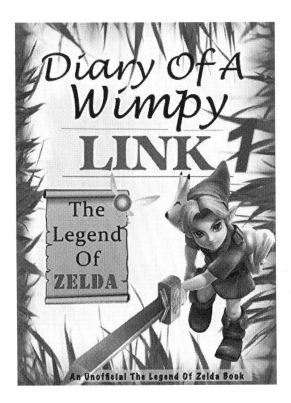

Have you Ever wonder what it would be like to be a Link? for Real?

Tap Here to download: http://amzn.to/2nd4Kp4

Paperback Edition here: http://amzn.to/2nUwMTl

Other Books by the Author

Minecraft: Star Wars "The Jedi Path"

Download here: http://amzn.to/1QVniSg

Download EP. 2 here: http://amzn.to/1pnlbx5

Download EP. 3 here: http://amzn.to/1t8Oq94

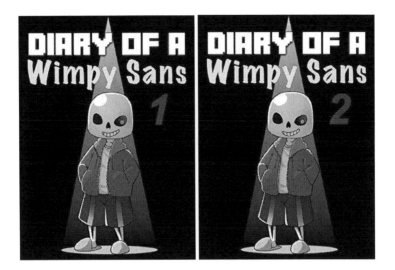

HAVE YOU EVER WONDERED WHAT HAPPENS TO SANS THE SKELETON AFTER *THE WAR BETWEEN HUMANS AND MONSTERS*?

SANS LEADS A COMFORTABLE AND SLUGGISH LIFE WITH HIS LOVELY BROTHER, PAPYRUS IN THE DEEPEST PART OF THE UNDERGROUND-VERSE.

EVERYTHING CHANGES WHEN SANS CAME ACROSS A HUMAN LOST UNDERGROUND.

WILL SANS KILL THE HUMANOID OR HELP HER RETURN TO THE SURFACE?

Get ready for fast-paced funny adventures complete with monsters and secret missions.

Printed in Germany
by Amazon Distribution
GmbH, Leipzig